Level UP:

Forging

Leodis

Games

Success

Neil Pritchard

First Printing 2023

Leodis Games Limited

Unit 10 Springfield Mills

Farsley
Leeds
LS285LY
UK

www.leodisgames.com

To Sue

Without whose help,
encouragement, and support.

Leodis Games would still be in my head.

And in memory of her mum Pat Milner
1946-2023 thank you for everything you
have done for us both over the years.

Acknowledgements

No one achieves anything alone.

I'd like to thank my wife, Sue. You have supported me from the beginning.

Simon Burdett, you believed in Leodis before anyone, including me, did. You pestered me to find a shop. And found the mill.

The rest of my shareholders. Dave O'Neill, Darryl Jones, James Clark, Jon Kerr & Richard Wilke. For putting your money where your mouths were when I needed it.

Tony Booth Lyndon for being more than just an employee. A friend, a mentor. The person who keeps me sane.

Scarlet King for helping me to edit the book.

And to you, my customers. Without you, Leodis would be nothing. Thank you for your continued support.

Introduction

There is a great irony in running a games store.

It's something that on the rare occasions I get to sit down with another store owner and I share it with them, they will nod sagely in agreement with me.

If you can manage to run a successful game store, you could instead run pretty much any other business you can think of.

And it would be easier.

You'd make more profit.

You'd spend less time on it.

And your quality of life would be better.

Running a game store is business on hard mode. This book explores some of the reasons why.

It's why I say the idea I had to set up a store is possibly the most stupid I've ever had. I'm seven and a half years in and I'm invested. I've put the time in. I've put the money in. I've put the effort in. Everything to make the store successful.

There is a reason for me to carry on running Leodis Games.

However, if I could go back again to that fateful day when I first made the decision, knowing what I know now, I wouldn't hesitate to choose something else. Something easier, something that wouldn't take up every waking moment for years.

I didn't always want to run a games store. I grew up in the back and beyond and when I first got into gaming in the early 90's I didn't even know that game stores existed, at least as we know them today.

Back then, within a 45-minute drive of home, there was a Games Workshop with its standard one table. Whenever I went in, there were always people who clearly knew the store manager, and they'd be playing a game. Across the nearby towns, there were two scale model and general hobby shops which also stocked some of the Games Workshop range.

And not knowing better, I just thought that was how it was. So, when I got back into gaming in the 2000s, I realised that a lot had changed. There were now dedicated stores - places you could go and play - places you could hang out with friends.

From the moment I understood this development, it was too late. The dreaded idea had spawned; "I'd like to run one". Fortunately, even back then, I wasn't naive enough to think I could just go out and set one up.

But the idea never left me. So, I spent about 10 years studying why it is that some games stores were successful, and some weren't. And that's part of what I write about in this book.

In the main, this book is the story of how Leodis Games came into being and how it evolved from that first rather stupid idea into the store it is now.

It's a peek behind the curtain. Showing how games store work, and I think anyone who has ever interacted with an independent games store will find interest in our story.

The second part of the book is more biographical. I recount the events and recall the lessons learned that led to me being the type of person who could set up a games store and make it succeed.

It's important context. I am convinced that if I went without those experiences, no matter how difficult or painful they were to struggle through, I would not be the man I am today and I would not be running a games store. Rather, I would be working in an office somewhere, quite possibly earning more money but with no desire, or inkling, of how to set out and work for myself.

And finally, the last part of this book is an exploration of why game stores fail. It's not a how-to guide; it's a how-not-to guide.

Why?

Well, even today I can look at a games store that has failed or is about to fail and tell you exactly why. But, even with all my knowledge and experience, I can't look at a successful games store and explain that success without diving into their data. I can make an educated guess could be made, but it would lack substance.

A games store is fragile. It can collapse under the pressure of a single fault. It can only thrive with the support of many varied successes; successes too numerous and nuanced to explain in a book such as this.

The only way I could explain all of it to somebody would be through one-to-one coaching. You can find my offer about that at the back of the book.

The way I've written the how-not-to guide is particularly blunt and abrasive. If you read it, and you take offence because you think I'm talking about you? Good, congratulations. I've just saved you from making a huge mistake. I wrote that part of the book in such a way for a particular reason.

As a successful games store owner people are always getting in contact and asking me for advice because they want to set up their own store. All too often, when I have given them that advice, they ignore it completely and decide that they know better than somebody who has experience and a proven track record in the industry.

They go ahead and set up a store anyway. They flounder, they fail, and they shut down.

I wouldn't wish the experience of a business failure on anybody. Particularly not a business like a games store, because it is a very public affair. Well, at least it should be. Everybody should know that you run it. Otherwise, how are you going to get customers? Everybody will know that you failed, and everyone will have an opinion on it. That will leave emotional scars that will take decades to heal.

If you're reading this, please believe me when I say that I don't want that for you. If you've ever considered running your own store, I beg you to read the whole book, particularly Chapter 9: Why

Game Stores Fail, more than once. And once you've read it, have an open and honest conversation with yourself. Do you recognise yourself in what I've described? If you do, don't do it.

You will regret it. It will be painful. And if you've read it and done it anyway, then I'm sorry but it will be your own fault.

For everybody else, however - everyone I've shown this book to so far has shared a melancholy smile and a sage nod when the book comes to discuss why games stores fail. They remark "Oh, yeah, remember So-and-So...", and recall how "Such-and-such store was like that..." because while I have generalised completely and I do not target any specific stores or any specific store owners, these patterns repeat time and time again. If you have frequented a few games stores in your life, there is a good chance you will see someone you know in them.

Finally, if you'd like a free copy of the eBook or audiobook, then see the offer over the page. I'll be shamelessly reminding you of the same offer throughout the book.

Stay Safe

Neil

Get the Audio & Ebook for Free

If you would like the audio version of this book, or it in a digital format then scan the QR code with your phone and follow the instructions on the website.

leodisgames.com/pages/level-up

The digital versions are free and easily accessible from your smart phone.

Prologue: A Stupid Idea

It's December 2016, and I find myself lying in bed in my parents' spare room on the Monday before Christmas. I had driven my mum and sister home the previous day after their weekend visit. Now, I have to prepare myself for the long journey back home. However, my mind is preoccupied with a debate I've been having for nearly ten years—I want to open a game store.

Deep down, I know it's a foolish idea. I've done the research. I've witnessed people proudly announcing their store openings on social media, only to quietly close them down within two years. Despite being aware of how ill-advised it is, I can't shake off the thought.

By that point, I'd spent seven years studying the reasons behind game store failures, learning all there is to know. I'd seen countless stores throughout the country open, struggle, and eventually shut their doors. Some closures have been amicable, while many owners have had their overinflated egos shattered by the harsh realities, leaving them mere shells of their former selves.

I'd seen others at events who had gone from stable jobs to failing stores, and eventually settling for menial work just to make ends meet. Slowly, they try to rebuild themselves financially and emotionally, yearning to regain their previous standing.

I'd also observed those who had to distance themselves completely from gaming, shutting out the hobby they once loved and isolating themselves from their friends as a coping mechanism for their failure—as if witnessing a dice roll may trigger some traumatic response in them.

Then there are those with darker tales of broken marriages, lost homes, and children growing up without a father. I was well aware that my idea was a foolish one.

Financially, it was a stupid idea. I lacked the capital to invest and heavily relied on my job at the time. I didn't have any wealthy relatives to turn to, and there was no chance my business plan would convince a bank to grant me a loan. My wife would never agree to use our house as collateral either.

Mentally, it's a poor choice. I was five out from a career as a forensic scientist, and although the emotional wounds were healing, the trauma of what I witnessed day in and day out still lingered. Some days, I'm fine, but others, I'm an emotional wreck. I'd made progress, but the road to recovery was slow and arduous.

Even to this day, I can't listen to any true crime stories related to cases I worked on. Yet, there I was, considering something that would undoubtedly add significant emotional stress to my already somewhat fragile state.

As I lie there, contemplating these thoughts, I realise I had gone through this internal struggle countless times before. I know the reasons why game stores fail (many of which are covered in this book). I've studied them extensively and can now identify potential failures in new store openings. I continue to evaluate any ideas I have against those reasons, and the results are far from encouraging.

Most scenarios don't end so catastrophically that I would lose the house—and I'm clever enough to immediately forget any ideas which might. They do end, however, with me experiencing a colossal failure, accompanied by the shame and embarrassment that follow. This shame often leads people to abandon gaming for years, if not forever. It affects them so deeply that they end up settling for positions well below their qualifications due to a loss of faith in themselves.

Yet, a new idea emerges. A new way of thinking about the problem. I try to reverse engineer my knowledge of why game stores fail to find viable scenarios that aren't doomed to fail.

How about a large gaming centre or store? It's a big space with plenty of tables. Somewhere people want to come and play... Starting at that size with my current means is untenable. It fails in 18 months if I'm lucky. Okay, so we start small. Something within reach, like a simple shop with no gaming space... It can't hold the stock needed. It might last two years, but no longer.

So, why even try to create something physical? This was back in 2016. The gaming market wasn't as mature as it is now. There was space, just, in the market for an online store to be viable.

I could position myself in a way that makes me stand apart from established stores. Services like Shopify weren't as wide spread as they are now, and it would take some ability to set up a website from scratch. That's a barrier to entry that, should

I be able to break through, would keep direct competitors at bay. I'd played around with web hosting before. I knew my way around cPanel. I could do it.

My internal meeting had concluded. I jumped off the bed. I headed home.

I was driving up the motorway on autopilot whilst I thought the details through. I reckoned I had twelve to eighteen months to make it work before other stores sorted their shit out online and diluted the customer base.

I began to consider what I'd actually be selling, and three distributors came to mind. One was Games Workshop, and they didn't (and still don't) supply to anyone without a physical store. That gave me the goal of setting up a small store within two to three years, using the online store as a springboard to do so.

Inspired, I pulled into a service station to email the other two. I explained my position and requested details on how to set up a retail account with them. I didn't really expect to hear back from either until at least a month later. I continued the drive home.

By my next stop, one had already replied to me with their order form. After a quick scan and some calculations, I could see that I can buy stock from them and sell it at a discount to make a small profit from each item while providing a reason to choose my store. The stock would sit in my spare room at home and I'd ship it out. I realised that this was starting to look doable.

I spent the remainder of the holiday setting up a website. As soon as January came, I put in a small order with my distributor. By the end of that first week of January, the store was live. A grand opening. Queue the fanfare.

I saw a single sale in January. It was a small start. But I had a business now, and it was time to get it growing.

Learning to Read

When and how did you learn to read? For most people you won't really remember. It will have been a process of going from not recognizing letters to eventually being able to read, taking several months, if not years. However, my experience was different.

I was there in school, that kid who the teachers ignored because I couldn't talk. I just couldn't figure out what these symbols on the page meant. While all the other kids in my class were reading books with sentences, I was sat with a book that had the same word on each page and a cartoon to illustrate that word. But it just didn't make sense to me.

The only experience I can compare it to in my adult life is when we went to Japan for a few weeks. Everything was written in Kanji, and there was no way for me to interpret it. It wasn't like looking at, let's say, French, where there are enough similarities between words to make out what's going on. Japanese is a completely different script.

Then, one Sunday night when I was eight years old, past the point where one should easily pick up reading, I sat with my mum. She had found one of the books my dad read as a kid, an Enid

Blyton book called "The Valley of Adventure" (yes, I know she's frowned upon these days, but this was the '80s).

My mum read it to me, and I wanted to know what was going to happen next. Suddenly, those symbols on the page made sense, and I could read. It was like a switch had been flicked. I left school on Friday unable to read books for five-year-olds, and when I returned on Monday, I was reading as well as anyone else in the class. Within six months, my newfound love of reading had put me ahead of most of my classmates.

Over the years, I've upset many primary school teachers and psychologists with this story. Some have even accused me of lying because they have been taught that you learn to read only one way. My story disrupts their beliefs on the subject.

It's always amusing to see someone take a piece of information that should be used as a guiding principle and turn it into a hardcore religious belief they're almost willing to die for.

This is one of the reasons I don't pay much heed to the people in charge. By the time I was eight years old, I had already realised that many were idiots. And as I got older, their incompetence has only become more apparent. But I'll delve into that later.

Chapter 1: The Little Shop

It began with that one sale, and started to slowly grow.

I quickly realised that the only leverage I had to expand the business was my time. I could work for free, allowing me to reinvest all sales back into the business. Additionally, my day job wasn't particularly taxing, which meant I could spend an hour or two each day engaging with customers and potential customers on social media. This is how you build a business in slow mode.

It's similar to playing mobile app games nowadays. You can play for free, but you have to invest time in activities you may not enjoy to earn the gold you need. Alternatively, you can spend some cash to purchase a bounty of gold large enough to make a pirate blush and accelerate through the game.

In the beginning, I didn't have that cash, and I was still learning the business. Slow progress worked for me. At the end of the first year, I could reflect on my sales graph and see a gradual increase over time. I even attempted to project future growth, but it turned out to be a laughably pointless exercise.

By September 2017, that slow rate of growth began to frustrate me. I could sense that I was almost there. Like a ship chasing another ship; success was always on the horizon, just out of reach. I knew that if I could figure out that missing piece of the puzzle, everything would level up like Mario eating a mushroom.

My hobby time had shifted from building and painting models to reading books and articles on business. It wasn't what I had envisioned when I set up the store, but the more I learned, the more I implemented. And the more I implemented, the more we grew, albeit still at a slow pace.

I'd love to claim that I mastered business in those two years, but even after seven years on this journey, I'm still learning. I've spoken to grizzled business veterans with over 30 years of experience, and they would tell you the same. They never stop learning; the day they stop is the day they retire.

Towards the end of 2017, I genuinely felt like I was gaining traction in the business. We were making a reasonable turnover each month, and we experienced our first significant increase in sales. When you examine sales over time in a business on a long enough timeline, it appears as a gradual upward trend. However, if you zoom in, you'll see periods of slow growth where you put in the work, followed by a massive jump, and then another phase of slow growth until the next leap.

I had experienced that first jump, and I wasted months trying to replicate it before realising that I needed to go back and put in more work, and refine more processes. I had a growing group of loyal customers, and we were starting to make a name for ourselves.

Back then, we positioned ourselves as the underdog, David against Goliath. We used a unique selling proposition (USP) that set us apart from our competition.

We weren't shit.

I wish I was joking, but I built the business based on that USP. In the same way, one of our current USP's is that we have clean toilets. Both of these should be standard for any business, but somehow in the gaming industry, it made us stand out.

I'd like to think that we played a part in eliminating the "we're not shit" USP as one you could use today.

Other stores saw what we did, understood they had to change, and became better.

However, the reality has more to do with the industry's maturation online. Unfortunately, that hasn't translated to physical stores yet. You can see that from the feedback I receive when someone visits another store for any reason—always complaining about the terrible state of their toilets!

By Christmas 2017, I had put in enough work to convince myself and my wife that this venture wasn't just a passing fad. I had found something I was willing and able to commit to, and I was determined to follow it through. The store wasn't my first attempt at running my own business to make money. For a while, I felt lost and unsure of what I wanted to do, frequently trying different things, knowing they weren't the right fit, and moving on to something else.

Looking back now, I can see that those years were spent figuring out what I didn't want to do and gaining skills along the way that became valuable once I found my calling. There's a phrase in business about an overnight success being years in the making, and this journey was part of that process for me.

In January 2018, I returned to work, knowing that if necessary, I could run the store full-time and pay the bills. It wouldn't be glamorous, and I wouldn't be rolling in money, but I could manage.

Having been unexpectedly made redundant from my job as a forensic scientist, a job that seemed secure on paper and should have been even safer during recessions when crime rates rise, was a wake-up call. I had a sense of relief knowing that I could rely on myself.

I also started paying attention to friends who kept asking when I would open a physical store. One of them had been sending me rental listings for months. I finally began considering them seriously, assessing if they were worth pursuing. Finding retail space proved to be a special kind of hell, and I was only partially committed to the search.

Around March, we came across a potential store. It was located in the student area of Leeds and had previously been a hairdresser's salon. After discussing it extensively with friends, we determined that the shop was far too small and in the entirely wrong location. However, there were around eight of us who were serious enough about opening a store in Leeds to consider investing money.

I had always imagined doing everything myself—building the business, opening the first shop, and eventually moving to a larger space. However, retail is a business that requires capital. You take money, invest it in stock, and earn a return when it sells. It's an illiquid business, making it challenging to raise a significant amount of money. Paying the bills each month was manageable because of the cash flow generated from stock turnover, but to grow, we needed to reinvest any profit into more stock.

I had been exploring options to raise capital outside of the business, which up until that point meant a business loan. It wasn't an idea I particularly liked. But now I had people willing to invest. People who were willing to put their money where their mouths were when they said Leeds needed a games store.

So, we actively began searching for a store. To this day, I'm still waiting for estate agents to return my calls about some of them. Fortunately, some estate agents weren't entirely incompetent, and they took the time to respond. We discovered that the store we were interested in had already been leased.

Then, Simon spotted a unit in a mill in Farsley that was available for rent. We made inquiries and arranged to visit. The following day, before work, we toured unit 10, which you might recognize as our current store number. It was perfect in every way except one— the price!

We took some time to consider it and determine if we could afford it. Two days later, after much soul-searching and calculating how much money we could personally contribute each month to cover the rent, I called the landlord back and informed him that we would take it.

That's when we received the disappointing news— the unit had already been leased. However, the landlord said he would let us know if anything else became available. Given my experiences with estate agents, I assumed this was just a polite way of saying we wouldn't hear from him again. But a few weeks later, on a Monday morning, I received an email from the landlord. The next day, we were touring unit 39.

Although smaller than the previous option, it was also considerably cheaper. We immediately agreed to take it. The question of when we could collect the keys arose, and I expected the answer to be several months away. To my surprise, the reply was "Friday."

Friday. That was three days away.

"Fuck."

I had assumed the process of renting a shop would be similar to renting a house, so I hadn't given much thought to the next steps. Acquiring the store had been the target, and the plan was to figure everything else out while waiting for the keys.

On that Friday, I left work, collected the keys, and headed to Ikea to buy a flat pack shop. I met with most of my (now) shareholders, and we purchased as many Kallax units as we could fit in our cars. We drove back to the store and spent the entire night assembling the units. Some of the units would serve as shelving for stock, while others would become the legs of our gaming tables. My Kallax gaming table design was a cost-effective and sturdy solution, at the perfect height for gaming, with additional Kallax units underneath for storage. Over the years, I've seen other stores copy our design.

We were tired but happy when we locked up the store at 9 PM and went to head home. We were less happy when we found that we had been locked inside the site. I called the landlord in a panic, and a security guard was dispatched to release us. On Monday, the landlord provided us with a key for the gates to prevent such fun incidents from happening again.

Saturday morning I woke up early, went to B&Q as soon as it opened, and had 18mm MDF boards cut into 3'x4' pieces. We returned to the store and finished assembling everything. By Monday, we had a fully operational store. The only thing left was to stock it.

Our main aim was to carry Games Workshop products. No company compares to them in terms of size and sales volumes in the wargaming world. Next to them, in terms of scale, was Wizards of the Coast and their Magic The Gathering products—but cardboard is a different beast to plastic.

Some may find it strange that Games Workshop insists on retailers having a physical store. However, in our increasingly digital world, this requirement prevents opportunistic individuals looking for a quick profit from undercutting brick-and-mortar stores. Additionally, having a physical store provides a space where customers can gather, socialise, and play the games they buy.

With our physical store established, I contacted Games Workshop to open an account. During the process, I had an interesting conversation with the representative who helped set it up. He informed me that a few months earlier, Games Workshop had changed its policy.

Previously, new stores received a 10% lower discount compared to established stores, with the possibility of earning the 10% extra within the first year by meeting certain criteria, such as a specified number of gaming tables and a minimum amount of time being open.

However, they discontinued this policy because they found that no new stores were making it to 12 months. They were all running out of money and closing before reaching that milestone. It added another reason to my list of why stores fail.

Our first Games Workshop order, complete with their racking, arrived that week. We opened the doors to the public on the following Saturday, ready to embark on this new chapter of our gaming store journey.

Get the Audio & Ebook for Free

If you would like the audio version of this book, or it in a digital format then scan the QR code with your phone and follow the instructions on the website.

leodisgames.com/pages/level-up

The digital versions are free and easily accessible from your smart phone.

Stuttering Through School

Unless you have one yourself, you probably haven't noticed my stammer. When I was a kid, it was severe—so bad that no one outside of my immediate family could understand me. It was worse than Colin Firth's stammer in "The King's Speech."

Growing up in a rural area in the 80s made school quite challenging with such a severe stammer. The other kids were generally fine, but the teachers quickly dismissed me as an idiot. It didn't help that I struggled with reading, and by extension writing, for a long time as mentioned.

I started seeing a speech therapist once a week when I was seven, and I continued therapy for four years. Here's a fun fact—with a bad enough stammer, you have no chance of saying "speech therapist".

Those years were incredibly significant in my life, not because they completely eliminated my stammer, but because they taught me the value of hard work and that achieving the seemingly impossible was within my reach. As a bonus, the therapy did mostly get rid of my stammer.

By "get rid of", as anyone who has experienced a stammer will know, I mean learning to manage and control it. Even to this day, when I'm very tired, I may experience word repetitions. Controlling my stammer still requires additional effort, and speaking can be tiring.

For me, talking is akin to playing chess. I'm always thinking a few words ahead of what I'm saying, carefully forming the words in my head before they leave my mouth. This process demands considerable mental energy. It's not uncommon for me to come home after a long day at the store, where I've been engaging in conversations, and simply sit quietly until bedtime. My brain becomes completely frazzled from the exertion.

However, my stammer is, in a way, my superpower. When speaking is challenging, you listen more than you speak. Any book on influence, building relationships, or effective communication will emphasise the importance of listening.

Talk less, listen more.

I've internalised this principle by default. Running the store is very much a people-oriented business, and being someone who is willing to listen has tremendously benefited me over the years.

Chapter 2: Growing

Looking back on it now, we shouldn't have opened so quickly. Instead, I should have taken a few weeks, maybe even a few months, and marketed the shit out of the store. However, this realisation comes with my current experience after spending a fortune on advertising. Back then, despite reading everything I could, I still lacked the experience.

One of the Catch-22s of setting up a store is that you need to run successful ads to attract customers, but you also need to run unsuccessful ads to learn how to create successful ones. Unfortunately, most people run out of money before figuring it out.

So, we opened with a little bit of fanfare. That Saturday, it was mostly good friends who called in to see how we were doing and to check out the place. It was enough to convince them to switch their game store preferences and place orders with us. We also had a few new customers come through the door in those first weeks.

For a while, it was a glorious experience, like the endorphin rush you imagine when you achieve a goal. However, reality soon set in, and it became a long, hard slog to grow the business. Starting without much capital meant we could only buy more stock with the money earned from the stock we sold.

The only reason we had money left over after paying the bills was due to two things: the extra 10% we were getting on Games Workshop sales (without which we would have gone out of business, I'm sure) and the fact that I was leveraging my own time and not taking any form of wage or payment from the store.

It was a slow-growth model, made even slower by the fact that I was still learning the business. Any mistakes with stock were costly. Everything would eventually sell, but there were cases where I would invest £50 into an item that sat on the shelf for 6 months before selling, giving me only £5 profit to reinvest. On the other hand, if I had invested the same £50 into other stock that sold a couple of times a month, I would have made £60 profit over the same period of time.

In our first week, I ordered what would become my white whale for a few years: an Akhelian Leviadon model for the Idoneth Deepkin.

It was their newly released centrepiece model, big and expensive. I thought that being the new release during our opening week, someone was bound to walk in and buy it.

It sat on the shelf for nearly 9 months before it sold.

If I had purchased 2 boxes of Space Marines instead of the Leviadon, I would have made sales every week during that 9-month period. It was a painful lesson to learn as a new business.

Nevertheless, we grew every month, and despite our initial fears, we always had enough money to pay the rent. The growth was slow, but other than time, running the place didn't cost me anything. I soon established a routine: leaving my day job, driving to the shop, packing mail and taking it to the Post Office, squeezing in a half-hour nap on the floor, opening up, and leaving at 10. Then, I would wake up at 6:30 the next day. I repeated this routine every Wednesday, Thursday, and Friday.

But it was worth it because almost every week we gained at least one new customer. Every new customer who entered the shop became a loyal customer, spreading the word about us and bringing in new people.

Nowadays, I have codified the strategies that make people want to come back to our store and even help us grow. I've even tried explaining these strategies to struggling store owners, but due to giving the information for free and their resistance to implementing my suggestions, it was often ignored, and their stores closed soon after.

Back then, it was more by luck than intentional design that I had the ability to listen to people and empathise with them. My stammerer naturally made me more of a listener than a talker, and in more ways than one, it helped me to grow.

By Christmas, we were joking about needing a bigger store, as the demand was exceeding our expectations. However, it wasn't until April that we took any action to address the need for a larger space.

The Fountain Pen

I attended a regular state-run high school, but it was unlike any other I had ever heard of.

The first and second years were located on a separate site from the rest of the school, which isn't too unusual. However, this site happened to be an old stately home dating back to the 16th century. Each classroom in the house boasted an ornate carved fireplace, and the walls were adorned with wood panelling.

Our woodwork classes took place in the old stables, and during playtime, we would venture out into the grounds. The science rooms were housed in a series of portacabins situated far enough from the main building to prevent any potential fire incidents.

It was in one of those science rooms that something happened, something that would change the trajectory of my life. Like most life-changing events, it was a small incident, but it had a profound impact.

It was during my second week at school when my chemistry teacher returned our first homework assignments. He informed me that he hadn't marked mine because my handwriting was abysmal and insisted that I redo it.

Now, most people faced with such a situation would likely consider two options: rewriting the assignment neatly or choosing not to do it and facing the consequences.

I, however, chose a third option.

That evening, on my way home from school, I stopped by Woolworths and bought a fountain pen. I then went home and rewrote the homework.

Being left-handed, a fountain pen is a terrible writing instrument. My first attempt resulted in smudged work. But that wasn't enough.

I rewrote it even faster, realising that the faster I went, the more illegible my writing became. The next day, I proudly handed in my homework to my chemistry teacher and simply stared at him. I suspect it was what my wife now refers to as my "psychopath death stare"—a look that silently challenged him, daring him to try me and see who would come out worse.

He didn't ask me to redo it again.

From that point on, I exclusively used a fountain pen throughout school, right up until my GCSE exams. Occasionally, a new teacher would suggest that I use a different pen, to which I would casually shrug, share the story, and leave it up to them to reconsider their request.

That experience marked the beginning of my "I don't take shit from idiots" attitude. It's one of the reasons I came to the realisation a few years ago that I'm essentially unemployable. However, it's also a significant factor in why I have been able to run a successful business.

In the hundreds of business books I've read over the past two years, I came across something that truly resonated with me. Unfortunately, I can't recall the specific book or author, but the sentiment was along the lines of: "Some people are meant to be employees, and that's perfectly fine. Some are meant to be employers, and that's okay too. The problems arise when they find themselves in the wrong role."

For the first 20 years of my adult life, I was an employee, and that was a problem for me. But as the boy who brought a fountain pen, it was an even bigger problem for my employers.

Chapter 3: The Big Shop

By April, it became clear that we needed more space. Our store was consistently full every night, and the shelves were overflowing, unable to accommodate any more stock. In less than a year, we had outgrown our small store.

On the one hand, it was a good problem to have, as it validated that I was on the right track. On the other hand, it presented a dilemma. We had reached a point where I could take a wage from the store, not a substantial one, but enough for me to live on.

I had been working over 90 hours per week between my day job, my time in the store & all the admin work to keep the store running. And it was taking its toll. If I chose to take a wage, we wouldn't be able to afford a move. Alternatively, we could move to a larger store and I would continue working exhausting hours for the foreseeable future. I struggled with this decision for weeks, going back and forth between the options.

The thought of working a comfortable 40-hour week in my own little shop was appealing, but so was the challenge and potential of a bigger store, even with the financial uncertainty it posed.

The decision kept me awake at night, and I sought advice from my shareholders and discussed it with my wife. Their counsel was helpful, yet contradictory, as neither option was inherently better nor worse, especially considering one option was completely unknown.

The younger version of me from ten years prior would have chosen the safe and cosy option of the small shop. However, I had grown since then. While part of me still longed for the safety, another part recognized that the truly safe option in this situation was working for someone else. Ultimately, I made the right decision.

I inquired with the landlord about larger spaces. As luck would have it, they had an available unit that we had previously considered but hesitated on and lost. Unit 10. It was a stroke of serendipity. We visited the unit one morning before work, and it appeared larger than I remembered. Part of the reason for this was the removal of a partition wall, and part was my adjustment to the size of the small shop.

The new unit was the perfect size. Initially, we hesitated because we were uncertain about our needs, but now I could envision gaming tables or retail shelving in the space currently occupied by sewing machines and cutting tables (as it was previously used by a bespoke curtain manufacturer). Without delay, we decided to take the new unit.

Unlike our previous move, this time the unit was still occupied, and we were given a relatively short notice of six weeks to plan the move. In a way, planning the move for the second time was easier. I was familiar with building tables and knew what type of shelving we desired. In fact, to this day, I can assemble Kallax units with my eyes closed.

However, we faced the challenge of moving an open store from one location to another, only 75 yards away in the mil, but still, it required moving all the stock, tables, and scenery. While we could afford to temporarily close the physical store, the online store had to remain open to ensure a steady income. Therefore, simply packing everything into boxes and dealing with sorting later, as one would during a house move, was not an option. I needed to know the location of each item of stock so that I could pack and ship orders efficiently, which meant keeping them on shelves.

The shareholders and I were privately discussing the logistics of the move, attempting to figure out how to accomplish it collectively. In the end, the solution was simpler than expected. When we informed our customers about the move, we were overwhelmed by their offers to help.

The day of the move became one of the proudest moments in running the store. Many of our customers showed up and assisted us. Some brought trolleys "borrowed" from their workplaces, while others offered their cars and vans. We formed a chain of people, walking and wheeling our stock and tables across the mill to the new location. Without their help, it would have taken us at least a week to complete the move. Fortunately, we managed to move everything on a Saturday. I spent Sunday setting up the store again, and we reopened on Wednesday. It was a day filled with a genuine sense of community, which has remained with the store ever since.

Reflecting back, I can now see that this move marked the beginning of what the store would eventually become, but more on that later. On that Wednesday, I left my day job, drove to the mill, and caught a brief half-hour nap on a different floor before opening.

I anticipated it would be a continuation of the previous year, but little did I know that everything was about to change.

The Boy Who Got A 'G' In Art

First, bonus points if you recognize the song. Second, I possess a GCSE certificate that indisputably proves my incompetence in art. I received the lowest possible grade, demonstrating that I am terrible at it.

To fail art, one must not complete the required work, yet I did the work and it was evaluated. Apparently, it was assessed by experts who attended university and studied art. So, why is this significant? Unlike those experts who ended up in academia because they couldn't earn a living from producing art, I spent over a decade producing highly detailed illustrations for court documents.

I was paid to draw! They were paid to tell me I couldn't. Furthermore, if you've ever seen any of the models I've painted, you'd know that I'm quite skilled at it. Maybe not at the level of winning competitions, but certainly good enough to make a living by selling my work.

Nevertheless, I possess a certificate that declares I am terrible at art.

Or perhaps, just perhaps, every expert who has passed judgement on your abilities was mistaken, and it's best not to heed their opinions.

Get the Audio & Ebook for Free

If you would like the audio version of this book, or it in a digital format then scan the QR code with your phone and follow the instructions on the website.

leodisgames.com/pages/level-up

The digital versions are free and easily accessible from your smart phone.

Chapter 4: Lockdown

We were now in the bigger store, and our stock, which had appeared substantial in the previous store, now seemed paltry on the new shelves.

We added more tables for gaming, bringing the total to 10. Back then, it felt like a significant number. Slowly but surely, more people started coming down in the evenings to play, and our community began to expand.

We transitioned from running small 8-player tournaments to hosting "big" 16-player events. Each event introduced us to one or two new customers. We were back in the cycle of leveraging my time for growth and reinvesting profits into more stock.

It's an odd feeling to look back on this point. I recall the move, but the subsequent 18 months remain a blur to me. I often claim that I worked 90-hour weeks during that time, but the reality is that it was probably even more demanding. According to Sue, I was becoming increasingly irritable, unreasonably angry, and experiencing disrupted sleep patterns. The strain was pushing me to the brink of a breakdown.

In December 2019, we decided to close the store the day before Christmas Eve and not reopen until January. Sue insisted that we take a break between Christmas and New Year's, but I wanted to stay home and work.

We ended up spending three days in the Lake District, where we did very little. It was during a walk from Bowness to Windermere that I realised I couldn't continue like this. Sue saw it too. It was destroying me.

I have no idea how our relationship survived those initial years. I was rarely home, and when I was, I either slept or had an insatiable desire to work more. But somehow, it strengthened our bond.

Sue had initially worried I wouldn't be able to make the shop work long term, which was why I hesitated to leave my job. However, we could both now see that I was making the store work. What replaced that concern, for both of us, was the impact it was now having on my mental health.

After running the numbers multiple times, I knew it was possible to pay myself a wage from the store, albeit a small one. The alternative was to continue on the same path, working tirelessly and potentially reaching a point where I could no longer run the store.

We agreed that it was time for a change. In January, I opened the store with the intention of running it full-time. I had planned to take two months to organise everything.

At the end of January 2020, I handed in my notice. Around the same time, news about a virus in China started to emerge. On February 28th, 2020, a Friday, I left my job. To commemorate this momentous occasion, I drove to the store, slept on the floor for half an hour, and then opened up as usual.

My plan was to take March "off" and operate the store as it was, essentially granting myself an additional 40 hours per week to recover. Then, in April, I would intensify my efforts to grow the business by investing more time, extending our operating hours, and increasing advertising.

By March, that virus in China was no longer just in China.

When you work over 90 hours a week, you don't really absorb the news. It's not that you don't see it; it permeates every aspect of our society. Although I haven't actively watched the news for over ten years, I can still provide a summary of current events.

However, working over 90 hours leaves little time to process the information. All I could gather was that everything would be fine and unaffected. That was the prevailing sentiment among the experts. Remember what I said about experts?

Then, on March 23rd, 2020, it became clear that things were not fine. The first lockdown commenced.

In the list of things I wouldn't want to occur during their first month of self-employment I had alien invasions, a domestic war, and the store burning down right at the top. Outside of those, I don't believe there are many other problems that trump a global pandemic which shuts the country down.

I remember sitting there after the announcement, feeling numb and in total disbelief. I released a few statements stating that we would remain open for online orders. The day before, Games Workshop had assured me that they would remain open no matter what. The next day, they called to say they were closing.

My main supplier of stock disappeared overnight, along with my primary source of income.

The shock of it all happening so suddenly left me somewhat unfazed. For some reason, I felt compelled to persevere, keep the store open, and trust that everything would somehow work itself out, even though I had no idea how.

The drive to the store on the first day of lockdown felt surreal. I was the only car on the road, carrying a copy of the store's council rates on the passenger seat, just in case I got pulled over by the police for breaking lockdown rules.

Arriving at the store without knowing what to do, I pulled out my phone and recorded a video, which I uploaded to our social media. I continued this practice daily throughout the lockdowns.

To my surprise, numerous people later approached me, expressing their gratitude and sharing how these videos helped them get through those challenging times. I packed the orders we received, handed them to the postman, and went home.

The following day, we had more orders, and this trend continued. By the end of the week, Dave, one of my shareholders, started coming down each day to help me. We engaged in socially distanced bickering while packing parcels, which kept us both sane. I had transitioned from working over 90 hours a week to spending only a few hours a day in the store. I needed to find something else to occupy my newfound time.

That's when I decided to focus on mastering marketing. Running a games store is undeniably challenging, with thin profit margins and little room for error. To succeed, one must excel in at least one of the fundamental pillars of business. The surge in new customers during the lockdowns was largely due to fortuitous circumstances.

However, retaining those customers, attracting more, and transforming them into loyal patrons relied on the hundreds, if not thousands, of hours and thousands of pounds I invested in learning effective marketing strategies during the lockdown.

I sought out marketers I admired and traced their influences upstream. Whenever they referenced other influential marketers, I pursued knowledge from them as well. I read books on advertising written in the 1920s, others which cost hundreds of dollars to buy, and invested hours in courses spanning the past three decades. I diligently practised everything I learned.

Have I mastered marketing? No. I will spend the rest of my life refining those skills. However, I am better at it than most business owners. In fact, I am more proficient than all the marketers who have attempted to sell me their services in recent years.

As March transitioned into April, the government began to relax lockdown restrictions. Games Workshop reopened, allowing me to replenish our stock. My daily videos mostly showcased our dwindling stock levels. By the time we received our first restock, the shelves were almost bare, except for an entire Sylvaneth army (they were so unpopular back then that not even the lockdown could entice anyone to purchase them) and a peculiar assortment of paints. Additionally, customers could now collect their orders from our door, adhering to the eased regulations.

The Introverted Extrovert

It's 8 o'clock at night, and all I want is to sit quietly. I've spent the entire day at a 40k tournament, and the store has been packed, completely full. 32 players from all over the country showed up to play three games of 40k, and it was a blast for everyone involved.

I've spent the entire day engaged in conversations with people, discussing their games, catching up with people I haven't seen since the last tournament, helping customers who wandered into the store, assisting someone with a new army, and offering guidance on paint choices.

Some conversations were with individuals I've come to know really well over the years. As an introvert by nature, being in constant interaction with others drains me. It's an additional effort to keep my stammer under control while engaging in conversation.

Right now, I feel completely exhausted. My brain is fried. I crave solitude, being alone with my thoughts. Instead, I've spent the entire day surrounded by people, and it takes a toll on me. Tonight, I will spend the rest of the evening not doing much, simply recharging mentally from the day's exertions.

I know that if I could get away with it, if Sue didn't remind me that I'll eventually burn myself out, I would gladly repeat this experience tomorrow and the day after that.

There's something truly enjoyable about organising and running these events, witnessing so many people having a fantastic time, even if it completely drains me.

Chapter 5: Community

The first day we opened for store pickups after the lockdown, I was filled with excitement to see people again. However, it soon became apparent that they were even more excited to see me.

When future historians write about the Covid pandemic and the resulting lockdowns, they will note that two health crises were unfolding simultaneously. One was the physical threat of Covid itself and the lives it claimed, and the other was the psychological toll inflicted by the lockdowns.

On that first day, and throughout the rest of the lockdown, I found myself standing on the store doorstep, engaging in conversations with people. These were individuals who had been isolated and had limited face-to-face interactions for weeks. Some lived alone and hadn't had a real conversation since before the lockdown. They were struggling, really struggling. So, I did what I could to help. I spent as much time as possible talking to them on the doorstep.

This experience not only benefited them but also reinforced an idea or rather a philosophy that had been brewing within me even before the lockdown. I had always recognized that we were a community of gamers, especially after the assistance we received during the store move.

However, it was during those early days of Covid that I truly understood the significance of our community. And since then, that understanding has continued to grow.

Occasionally, news outlets will publish articles about wargaming, particularly highlighting the success of Games Workshop. While they rightfully attribute the growth in customers to the lockdowns, I haven't come across any that explain how these customers have been retained after lockdown.

What I began to realise, standing on that store doorstep, was that we are increasingly living in isolated, digital worlds. We work from home, socialise online, and even seek out romantic partners through our mobile phones.

In contrast, wargaming is an analogue and face-to-face activity. When you and I sit down for a game, we agree to spend a certain amount of time interacting socially with each other. This is what has sustained the popularity of gaming beyond the Covid era and will continue to do so long after I have sold Leodis and moved on.

Since that first day on the doorstep, witnessing the trauma experienced by individuals due to their enforced isolation, I have made that human connection the driving force of the store.

But of course. The government kept getting in my way.

Get the Audio & Ebook for Free

If you would like the audio version of this book, or it in a digital format then scan the QR code with your phone and follow the instructions on the website.

leodisgames.com/pages/level-up

The digital versions are free and easily accessible from your smart phone.

Back to Gaming

Like many people, I started gaming when I was young, around 1990. It all began when someone at school lent me a copy of White Dwarf magazine.

This was during the release of the Realm of Chaos books, if you remember them. That particular issue of White Dwarf was focused on Nurgle, the Chaos god. As I read it, I became absolutely hooked. The combination of grotesque and comedic elements, along with the description of Nurgle as the carnival of chaos, captivated my 12-year-old self.

I began my gaming journey, or rather, my collecting journey, from the age of 12 until I was around 15. I had third edition Warhammer Fantasy and Rogue Trader for Warhammer 40k, and I loved them. I remember that at one point, I knew the entire Rogue Trader rulebook by heart because I had read it so many times.

However, like most people, I grew up and fell out of love with the hobby. I discovered beer and girls, and my interests shifted. It wasn't until 2006 that I found my way back to the world of gaming.

At the time, I had been working as a forensic scientist for about five years and was under immense stress. Looking back, I can now see how the job indoctrinated you like a cult. Starting with minor cases, I gradually worked my way up to more serious ones, including assaults, rapes, and murders.

By the winter of 2006, I was incredibly stressed, though I didn't fully comprehend it at the time. It was only years later, after being made redundant, that I realised the impact it had on my mental health. However, Sue, my wife, could see how much it was affecting me at the time, and she understood that I needed something to take my mind off the stress.

That's when she made what I jokingly refer to as possibly the worst decision of her life.

Back then, Hobbycraft in the UK stocked part of the Games Workshop range. Whenever we visited the store, which was quite often due to Sue's many hobbies, I found myself drawn to the Games Workshop section, gazing at the models.

Then, just before Christmas, she had had enough. She told me to pick a box, and that would be my Christmas present. I chose a box of Warhammer 40k Orks, specifically the Ork Boyz that are still available today. She also got me one of the starter paint sets, which I still have some of the paints from, and the clippers, which are still with me, though they don't get much use these days. I don't remember it, but she must have also bought me some plastic glue because I quickly assembled the Ork Boyz after Christmas. And just like that, I was hooked again.

I vividly remember a few days into the New Year when it heavily snowed, and I ended up not going to work. I have always hated driving in the snow, especially since the incident when I drove off the side of a cliff and almost killed myself. But that's a story for another day.

Despite the snow, I drove Sue back to Hobbycraft, pretending she wanted to get something, but in reality, I wanted to pick up the Ork Codex.

By February or March, I had amassed around 1000 points of Orks, assembled if not painted. I started looking for a place to play and googled war games clubs in Leeds. That's when I discovered the Leeds Night Owls, a war games club that still exists today. Despite not having been in many years, I still consider myself a member.

They met every Thursday night and Sunday morning in Headingley. The first few sessions were challenging for me because I was painfully shy and introverted at the time. However, I pushed through, kept going back, and gradually made friends. I had fun.

It's worth mentioning that I had moved to Leeds in 2000 when Sue got a job at a school, so I didn't really know anyone in the area. When my job was particularly horrific, which it tended to be more than not, the friendships I formed through gaming, and the games themselves, became sources of comfort which got me through.

They distracted me from what I was doing. I would think of what list to take to my next game, or what army I might dive into next. These friendships and the games we played carried me through some really tough points in my life.

So, when I was finally made redundant, the first thing I did on that Friday was drive home, change, grab a bag and my army, pick up a couple of friends, and head down to Warhammer World for what would be the last independent tournament held there.

That Saturday night became infamous as the "cards of death" night, where someone who now holds a high position at Games Workshop managed to wreak havoc on their bathroom plumbing due to excessive vomiting. But that's also a story for another time.

I share all of this to emphasise how much gaming has meant to me over the years. Part of the reason I established Leodis Games was to give back to the community and hobby that has brought me so much joy.

It's also why we operate the way we do, maintaining a laid-back and welcoming atmosphere, eager to help newcomers and introduce them to the hobby. This stems from my own tentative steps back into the hobby, which could have easily gone in a different direction, leading me never to return.

Chapter 6: Growing the Community

We finally reopened the shop, although gaming was still not allowed. At least we could let people in through the door. It's surreal, writing this in 2023, that just three years ago I couldn't allow people into my games store... to play games.

Regardless, we made the most of the situation. I remember using pink duct tape to mark arrows on the floor, guiding people on which way to go. They politely waited at the entrance for the person before them to finish. Looking back now, it all seems sort of comical.

At the time, people were saying that their grandkids wouldn't believe it in 40 years. I believe it won't be long before we struggle to remember that we actually did it.

I had gone full-time in the store at possibly the worst moment in history, but somehow I made it work. As people realised how popular gaming had become and were stuck at home bored, new stores started popping up everywhere. However, I don't know a single one that is still around today. They all went out of business one way or another.

We put in the work, opening every day, sorting mail, speaking to customers, and listening to them. On dry days, people even started garden gaming as soon as households were allowed to mix outdoors. There was a desperation to play, to be face-to-face with another human.

I remember having conversations with friends during that year about locking ourselves in the store for a game. No one would know, and it wouldn't hurt. I knew how much some of them were struggling mentally and how much gaming would help them.

But I said no every time. It wasn't just about the legality; it was about doing the right thing. I felt like I let them down when the details of the Tory Partygate scandal came to light. But at that point, it seemed like everyone was doing the right thing.

Eventually, summer arrived, and restaurants were allowed to reopen. I took that as a cue to open up gaming as well. We started with just four socially distanced tables and gradually increased to eight.

In October, I had a chance conversation with Tony, realised he was looking for a part-time job, and hired him on the spot. It gave us the opportunity to open more days and further grow the store.

Tony managed a few days of work before the second lockdown hit, and we had to part-furlough both of us. It felt like we had just started building up the store, only to have it taken away from us again.

But this time, the number of people coming to the store to play games had grown, and our WhatsApp gaming groups had expanded. This was when it truly became a real community.

We were all in it together, supporting each other through painting competitions, uplifting one another during low moments, and celebrating each other's successes. The legacy of Leodis Games will be its community long after I'm gone, and I'm not sure it would be what it is today without being forged by the lockdowns.

Eventually, spring arrived, and most people had been vaccinated, leading to the easing of restrictions. We were able to bring back gaming and even add a few more tables. Then came the end of restrictions totally, Johnson's so-called "freedom day". We opened at midnight and had people playing until 6 in the morning. We made the papers.

Get the Audio & Ebook for Free

If you would like the audio version of this book, or it in a digital format then scan the QR code with your phone and follow the instructions on the website.

leodisgames.com/pages/level-up

The digital versions are free and easily accessible from your smart phone.

Appearing on BBC One.

Picture the scene if you will.

Monday morning, I've just got back into work after a week on holiday. I've gone into the lab and fully togged up. Lab coat, face mask, mob cap & gloves. Completely covered up to prevent me from putting my DNA onto anything by accident or to prevent anything that's particularly nasty in the lab from hurting me.

And I'm sat at the computer checking my emails. There are a lot of them. I've been away for a week. It's the civil service. People like to send a lot of pointless emails. So I'm there working my way through and the phone rings.

It's reception and they've got a message for me. They've phoned to let me know that the film crew are running late, so they're not going to be there for about another hour.

At this point. I stop checking my emails. I turn around in the computer chair and ask everybody else in the room.

"So is there anything anybody wants to tell me?"

There were a lot of sheepish looks. And eventually somebody confesses. They'd all been asked the week before to do a demonstration for TV. They'd all chickened out of it. And as they put it, you will talk to anyone so we thought that you wouldn't mind.

I've just been told that in just over an hour I'm speaking to a film crew. That wasn't what I had planned for Monday, but I can deal with it. So my next question is,

"Which room have you sorted me to do it?"

To this I get lots of silence.

"So you did get a room for this, didn't you?" I ask.

"You did realise I can't do this in the lab? Because if I do, we'll have to completely deep clean it. Shut it down. Take swabs. Send them off to be processed to prove that the room is completely DNA clean before we can start using it again.

One of you have sorted me out with one of the non DNA clean rooms that has a fume cupboard so I can do this?"

Again, Utter silence.

This wasn't what I wanted to walk into the first day back after holiday. Cue a frantic hour, running around trying to find a room. Which is hard because most of the rooms where we have fume cupboards are designed for DNA work.

Eventually our drugs department agrees that I can use their Bulk room. Which is the room they only use if they get the type of drug consignment that turns up on a HGV with a police escort.

Great.

There's only one problem. Because it's not in use, it's their store room. So I spend a frantic 20 minutes hiking all sorts of equipment out of the room and piling it into their main room. Much to their disgust and complaints.

But I now have a room.

Then I'm running around trying to find stuff I can use to demo. I can't use anything real. I can't use a real case. So I have to go and raid the training store. Fortunately we've got stuff that somebody had set up for some training that hasn't happened yet.

I grab that and I grab all the chemicals and equipment I need.

Then, the hard part. I have to run around and try and find one of the only two proper cloth lab coats in the building that actually has the Forensic Science Service logo embroidered onto the top pocket.

Because we never use them. We always use disposable lab coats because we literally have to get rid of them after each and every case we do. And quite frankly some of the stuff we get on it isn't coming out at a 90 degree wash.

So, about five minutes before the camera crew turned up. I'm completely frazzled. But I have everything.

They arrive and then the nightmare begins.

If you've never dealt with a camera crew and presenter it's not fun.

The director thinks he Steven Spielberg. The presenter thinks they're whoever the current biggest draw on primetime TV is. When in actual fact, they're just two plebs hired to do a job.

Cue multiple takes. Cue me having a stand up argument with the director, that no I was wearing my full getup whilst doing the talk. Even if the presenter was just going to stand there and watch in what she turned up in. Because, one that's how we worked. And two I didn't want any of my neighbours knowing what I did for a living.

So a two and a half minute piece of TV took over two and a half hours of faffing around.

But eventually it's done. I've got them out my hair. It takes me the rest of the day

to tidy up. Move everything back. Get rid of everything that I need to dispose of.

At the end of the day I finally finished checking my emails.

Then the next night, I'm sitting at home. I don't know why because we hardly ever watched the TV. But we had the news on and then it got to seven o'clock and it swapped to The One Show. Which I'm not sure if it's currently on air was the BBC's primetime current affairs programme at the time.

And lo and behold, there's an article about the work of the Forensic Science Service and what they're doing on cold case sex crimes. So we sit and we watch it

There's an interview with one of my more senior colleagues about the processes involved.

And then there's my two and a half minutes of fame. We sit and watch it. Then afterwards Sue turns to me and says says.

"Do you know that person?"

I've managed to disguise my identity so well, with my regular day to day get up in work that even my own wife didn't recognise me on the TV.

And I now have a claim to fame that I'm the only person ever to have said the words semen and ejaculation on BBC One at 10 minutes past seven on an evening.

Chapter 7: Freedom to Game

Restrictions ended, and we were able to resume organised play in the store. We ran tournaments and slow grow leagues, and the store came back to life. We had spent 18 months building an online community of people who wanted to be offline, and now they could come down and play. The energy and buzz in the store were incredible. Tournaments were selling out, and we were consistently full most evenings.

However, I soon realised that we had run out of space once again.

I discussed the issue with my shareholders and the landlord, and we came up with solutions. The landlord knocked down a wall that separated our D&D room from an unused office, giving us an extra two tables.

But I wanted more. I wanted 16 tables, as having players in multiples of eight is important for Swiss seeded events and reaching the "proper" tournament league. The closest place that could offer that kind of level was in Manchester.

I had a conversation with a customer who worked in the building trade, and he suggested moving the counter and removing the storage behind it. I had been struggling with the space issue for months, but he approached it with fresh eyes and expertise in making spaces work.

That Sunday night, armed with power tools, some shareholders and I transformed the store. A few hours later, we had the space for three additional tables. The next day, on the August bank holiday, I went to Ikea and walked out with the ingredients required to create three more table bases using my Kallax recipe. The table tops were delivered the following day, and by Thursday, we had a store with 16 tables.

By the end of September, we were successfully running 32-player events. We had levelled up once again.

We also established a standing agreement with the landlord that we would be the first to know if anything larger came up on-site.

While I've intentionally written the business advice side of this book as a how-not-to guide, here's an observation that can be helpful to anyone starting a business: When you have an idea that you know will work, implement it quickly, usually within hours, or in the case of larger projects like knocking down walls, within days.

Some people may think you move too quickly, but those who work for themselves and have their income tied to results understand the need for speed. Take that information and see if it works for you. If it does, run with it, and you might go far.

Moving into October we were now operating with 16 tables and growing rapidly. In December, I hired Scarlet and we started opening properly on Mondays.

As 2022 arrived, we were doing well by every metric I could measure. I started to believe that I had finally achieved success with the game store.

Then, Russia invaded Ukraine, triggering a cost of living crisis. Inflation and interest rates soared, and our suppliers faced significant supply issues. But that's a story for another day, and I will leave it for another time.

Fun with Kickstarter

I think I may hold a strange record with Kickstarter because, as far as I'm aware, I'm the only person in the games industry who has ever run two Kickstarters with delivery of physical products, and they arrived before the date specified in the Kickstarter campaigns.

If you've ever backed anything on a crowdsourcing website, you'll know that the usual experience involves months and months of updates and apologies from the creators, explaining why things have gone awry.

So, partly because I wanted to demonstrate that timely delivery was possible if one truly wanted it, and partly because I wanted to try out the entire process myself, as at that point I had coached and mentored more than one person through their own successful Kickstarters. And I had also told more than one person that what they were planning wouldn't work, only to see them follow through with it and have it collapse around them anyway. It would be a good experience to do it myself.

I decided to run a couple of Kickstarters for Board Matz, which were PVC gaming mats we sold at the time.

Both campaigns were successful, with funding achieved in under an hour, and they introduced me to new customers.

However, I also encountered some of the wonderful quirks of Kickstarter. For the second campaign, I found a printing company in the US that could produce the same type of mats, allowing me to ship to both the UK and the US. This led to the need to explain to backers from Canada why I was only shipping to the US when I said I was only shipping to the US.

It's worth noting that, unless they have made changes in recent years, Kickstarter does not provide a way to block backers by country. This can be really annoying, as there will be many instances where backers from unsupported regions may request exceptions.

So it's not unusual to have to refund somewhere between one and five percent of your backers when you realise that they're in parts of the world where shipping is practically an impossibility.

Running these two successful Kickstarters taught me valuable lessons, which have proven helpful when advising others interested in launching their own campaigns. If you're considering running a Kickstarter project, I encourage you to check out my coaching offer at the back of this book.

Get the Audio & Ebook for Free

If you would like the audio version of this book, or it in a digital format then scan the QR code with your phone and follow the instructions on the website.

leodisgames.com/pages/level-up

The digital versions are free and easily accessible from your smart phone.

Chapter 8: Why game stores fail

If you just want the story of how Leodis Games came to be, you've got it, and you can skip these chapters. If you're here because you want to run a games store, they are essential reading.

Part 1: Why This Wouldn't Work Now

When I first started, there were several factors that contributed to our success that are no longer applicable today.

Back then, Amazon Prime was still in its early stages, and the expectation of next-day delivery hadn't been ingrained in customers' minds.

The entry into the online market was more challenging at that time. It has become much easier for anyone to set up an online store.

Online advertising was not as prevalent or sophisticated as it is now. We didn't face the same level of competition and noise that businesses encounter today when trying to reach their target audience effectively.

If you Googled "games stores" back then, you would get a limited number of results, perhaps only a few pages. However, now there are hundreds of results for the same search, making it more challenging to stand out among the competition.

Many existing stores at the time were just not that impressive. Most of them had started as online-only businesses and transitioned into physical stores. Customers didn't question buying from individuals operating out of their bedrooms.

All of these factors allowed me to start as I did, and today that just wouldn't be possible. If you were to try and repeat my process today you'd have somewhere between 6 months and 2 years where the outlook would be hopeful. Your sales would slowly increase and your business would slowly grow.

But eventually you'll realise you're never going to hit the numbers you'll need to be successful. By which point you've already invested significant time & money into running a failed venture.

If I were starting from scratch today, I would do something else entirely.

If you're interested in the specifics, I encourage you to check out my coaching offer at the end of the book.

Why game stores fail

Part 2: Personality Traits

This is a difficult chapter to write. There's no way to talk about someone's personality traits without running the risk of upsetting them.

So please understand that if you are upset by this, I haven't deliberately set out to offend, but I have set out to have an honest conversation about why some people are suited and why some people aren't suited to not just running a game store. But to really any form of business.

And everything you will read in the strategy part of this book about why stores fail is compounded upon by these various personality traits.

With all these traits, it's a lot easier to look and see this in other people than it is to see it in yourself. Part of human nature is we're quick to see flaws in others. We're slow to see them in ourselves.

It may be worth if you are considering setting up your games store to read about these traits and first, see if you can spot them in other people. Before looking at whether you can spot them in yourself.

Employees vs Business Owner

Nobody is a 100% one way or another, but everybody skews towards one. And most people by quite a large margin to being either an employee or an employer.

And this works both ways.

I spent 20 plus years working for other people and I really should not have. As anybody who's ever had the misfortune to manage me in a business will tell you. I'm pretty much unemployable.

And the reason for this is that the things that make me good at running my own business.

Being able to make quick decisions, being able to ignore what other people say and do what I know is right. Being able to run completely counter to public opinion.

These are all excellent traits for running my own business. They are terrible traits for being an employee.

But most people skew towards employee.

If you're somebody who should be an employee. if you're somebody who is going to be happiest in life working for somebody else. And you go out and you set up your own business you will be constantly looking to other people for advice, for guidance, to tell you what to do.

And in part the entire business coaching world, which to a small extent I'm a part of, exists because there are people who need to be told what to do all the time.

If that's you then you will be adding a lot of unnecessary stress into what is already an incredibly stressful situation. Anybody who tells you that running a business is easy. Especially if they want to sell you a seven point plan is clearly lying.

It is a hard thing to do.

Much harder than to work for somebody else.

And you can see this because a lot of people who have attempted to run game stores or any other businesses. When they fail at the business that they are doing.

Then they go and get a job and work for somebody else.

And if you look. At least 80% of people, and more likely 90% plus, who fail at starting their own business. End up back in the world of employment. And are much happier for it.

The other 10% of people. That's who should be running their own business, who if a particular business fails. Well, they would do what I would.

If I got up tomorrow and something had happened that meant Leodis Games was no longer a viable business. I've already got five or six other business ideas up my sleeve, to turn my hand to. To be back up and running something else. Because the idea of going and working for somebody else. Of going back to being employed is alien to me.

It just wouldn't work and I know it wouldn't.

So this personality trait, just compounds everything else.

And I've seen many people over the years who tried to set up their own game store. And the fundamental reason that it failed was they were waiting for somebody else to tell them to do. To tell them what they should do next. Something went wrong. They wanted somebody to tell them how to fix it.

And that's not how the world of business works.

Delayed Gratification

If you've never read about the marshmallow experiment with young children, google it.

Business is the art of delayed gratification.

For instance. I'm currently writing this book. I get nothing from that today.

I'll get some pay off when I publish it. But I'll slowly get more over time.

That's in part why so many people start books but don't finish them.

Employment on the other hand is instant gratification. You turn up for your allotted hours. And get paid at the end of each month.

There are some long term strategies in my business that I've been working on for over a year, that I don't expect to pay off for at least another year.

If you can't do that then you will struggle to grow any business long term.

A Strong Dislike of People

I am always amazed at the amount of people who decide that they want to set up a games store who don't like other people.

And I know this sounds obvious.

But I've seen so many people fall into this trap. They don't like other people. They don't like spending time around people they don't know. They'll go and game with a group of friends. But don't want to spend time with complete strangers. They don't want to have random people coming and talking to them about their hobby. Or just about the world in general.

I've seen many people over the years who have started games stores with this attitude and of course there's a problem with this.

If you don't want to interact with people. If you don't want to deal with people. They very quickly get the message. And realise they're not welcome. And given that a games store is more about building a community than it is about putting stock on a shelf.

It will significantly impact on your ability to stay open.

To give you a personal example of this.

I know a lot of teachers. I've worked in a school for nearly seven years. And every one of those teachers at some point has told me to consider retraining as a teacher. The reason being that I'm very knowledgeable about the subject I'd teach. I understand it, I've got a good grasp of it. I can easily explain it.

Which you would think would make me the perfect candidate.

But I know I can't stand children. I find teenagers pathetic, whiny and annoying. So on the one hand, I've got all the skills I need to be a really good, efficient teacher. Except I'm lacking the most important one. Because any good teacher will tell you that teaching is all about building relationships. I have no interest in building those relationships. I have no interest in interacting with children.

So I'd be a really poor teacher. I very quickly realised that wasn't a career I wanted to follow. If I had I'd have been awful at it.

I'd have hated it

Now imagine you replace teacher with games store owner and you replace children with customers?

And you end up with the same results. That's not going to work out well for anyone involved.

Following on from this is another trait that I've observed in games stores that fail and this is the person who always wants to be right.

Again, with this one, there's no there's no good way of talking about this without potentially upsetting you. Although if this is your personality then you're not likely to be upset. Because you'll automatically assume that I'm wrong and that you know better.

This comes back to community building. To being a place that your customers want to come to.

If you're the type of person who when someone wanders into your store mentions it's a lovely day because they can see so much blue sky. And you just have to correct them and tell them that the sky isn't blue because you need to be right all the time.

You're going to turn those customers away. And that if that is your personality, well you can mask it

Any of these personality traits you can if you want to control. You can suppress them. But eventually you'll reach a point where you can't do that.

And as soon as you start putting a load of stress into the mix. As soon as you start putting in the constant pressure of running your own business. It's likely that very quickly you'll be too preoccupied with that to control any personality trait that you have. It'll start coming back out and you'll start putting off customers.

And in the games store you live in you die by your loyal customers. It's as simple as that. And if you have a personality that means you can take somebody who would be loyal and make them want to go elsewhere. You are going to really struggle.

Lazy vs Hard Working

Again, something you can easily observe in others. And then maybe question if it's something that exists in you.

Are you naturally lazy?

Or are you naturally a hard worker?

Whichever you are will be amplified by being your own boss.

I've talked elsewhere about working 90 plus hour weeks to get the store up and running. If I stopped and recorded everything, I'm probably still at 70-80 hour week most of the time.

I may only work 2 days a week physically in the store. And that's what the lazy person sees. And wants for themselves.

But I'm always working. Always reading up on business. Listening to courses. Planning out where I want the business to go. I'm going on holiday in a few months and that'll mean I drop down to maybe 20 hours work that week.

The lazy person reads that and labels me a workaholic so they don't have to feel bad about not doing it.

And then tries to do the minimum amount of work that can get away with.

And when you're the boss you can get away with very little. Until that is the bills come due.

The Big Ego

I could also call this being overconfident.

In business you need an ego. You need the confidence to carry on doing what you know is right. No matter what others are saying.

But there's a fine line. You need enough humility to consider advice from others.

There are many examples of when I've been told to do one thing and I've done the opposite because I knew it would work. And people always remember these.

There are also many times when I've considered the advice I've been given and followed it because it was sound. People won't remember these.

Money

And finally, I'd like to talk about money.

There are two sides to money that can really affect a business's chance of success. First, let's talk a bit about personal finance.

Since the day that I went full time, I have been able to pay myself a wage every month. And pay myself enough a wage to keep my household budget ticking over. That's not been a problem for me.

But in part that's because over the course of the last seven years, my wife and I have made decisions that have helped us to have a relatively low household budget.

We don't have a massive mortgage. We bought a house well over 20 years ago and we've nearly paid it off. We don't have huge car loans. We don't have extravagant lifestyles. So we can have we can have a very comfortable living on a relatively small wage.

If you're currently in a job that pays you a good wage. If you're somebody who earns a lot of money. You almost certainly have the lifestyle of somebody who earns a lot of money. And your family almost certainly has the same lifestyle.

Which means if you start a store and immediately slash your income. Because that's the only way you can make the games store viable. Certainly in the first two to three years and possibly for longer than that. You're going to have massive issues.

Because you'll have the lifestyle of someone who earns a lot more than you currently do. And your family will be used to that lifestyle. That will cause a huge amount of stress.

And you only need to go and find somebody who has ended up having to leave a well paid job and get a significantly less well paid job. And talk to them, to find out how much stress that will put on your family. It's the type of stress that causes divorce.

Starting your own business is up there in the top five most stressful things you can do. And breaking up a family is up there in the top five most stressful things you can do.

So you can end up putting yourself into huge amounts of stress. And I know many an individual who were competent enough to make their business work over time. Who have had to make a choice. It's either the wife and the kids or the store.

Most people in that situation. choose the wife and kids.

Then they close the business. They go and get themselves a job very similar to the one they were doing before. Very similar pay to the one they were doing before and they're much happier because of it.

These are the people I talked about in the first chapter. Who can quite amicably wind up the business. But although it's a good decision for them. It's still stressful closing down a business. It's still a huge amount of stress that they've got on their marriage.

And it certainly makes it much less likely the next time you have a business idea that you're going to get any form of agreement from your family to go with it.

This closes a lot of businesses not just games store.

And then the next thing to talk about with money. Again this is a this is a very personal one.

Everybody reading this will know at least one person who, be it in their own business. Through the business they work in, through running a charity, through a family inheritance, winning the lottery or some other means. Find themselves in the possession of what they consider to be a large amount of money.

And they've just gone weird.

Often weird enough to end up in jail for fraud or embezzlement.

On paper money is just that. It's paper.

Emotionally it's got a lot of powerful feelings associated with it. And some people can't handle those emotions.

They've taken money that wasn't theirs. They've spent money that they should have saved. They've destroyed relationships. And ended up in a lot of trouble. Because they couldn't cope with the emotions of having money.

Now if you run your own business, if you run your own games store. You should in a month, have more money passing through your business account than most people will earn in a year. Because if you don't, you're not going to last for long.

But of course, I can have this conversation with you now. And we can intellectually agree that that money isn't yours. And it's not even the businesses because most of it is to pay for stock, rent, amenities, or pay wages. And it's only after all that stuff's been paid out, at the end of the month, that anything that's left over becomes your profit.

For some people, when they look at their stores bank account. They see that money. They have this weird reaction.

They become like Gollum with the One Ring.

And then they get themselves into all sorts of trouble. For some in the first month they just end up taking the lot and just disappearing with it. For most it's more subtle than that. It's taking a little bit of money out each month, because you deserve it. You're working hard. And then one month you've taken far too much out and you can't afford to pay the bills and the business must fold.

It's a very common occurrence. As I say. You will almost certainly know of at least one person who's done it at some point in their lives. You probably know many if you sit down and actually think about it.

And if you've never had a huge amount of money at any point. Then you don't really know how you will react to it. Until the time comes and it's too late.

If you then take this weirdness around the money and combine it with the fact that you should be an employee not an employer. Which means that because there's nobody looking over your shoulder, you're even more likely to take that money. And then you add it to the fact that you're naturally lazy. So you won't put in the work you think you'll put in to make the money back next month. And you can see how all these traits compound on top of each other.

And don't get me wrong. I don't think any of these traits make you an inherently bad person. I don't think the opposite of these traits make you an inherently good person. I can show you good and bad people who have all these traits to a greater or lesser extent.

But I do think that they make it hard for you to run a successful business. And given that running a games store is business on hard mode.

It makes your chances of being successful very slim.

Get the Audio & Ebook for Free

If you would like the audio version of this book, or it in a digital format then scan the QR code with your phone and follow the instructions on the website.

leodisgames.com/pages/level-up

The digital versions are free and easily accessible from your smart phone.

Why Games Stores Fail

Part 3 Business Fundamentals

In this chapter I'll talk about some of the fundamental things I've seen people get wrong over the years so that you may have a chance to look at them and hopefully not do them.

Money

I ended the last chapter with money and I'll begin the this chapter with money as well, but in a different way.

I've talked about how I set up with zero capital. I've also explained why you can't do that today. But I'll say it again. That will not work today. The market has matured, there are too many other stores. The things I got away with seven and a half years ago. You will not get away with now.

So knowing what I know now. If I was crazy enough to think that I would set up another game store the first thing I would be looking at was my funding.

There's only one other book that I know of about setting up a games store. It's by Gary L Ray. And in it he shows a calculation for what you need for your first 18 months in terms of money. And he estimates 150 grand. Now that book was written in 2018, so that's written 2018 BC (before COVID).

And a lot has changed since then. I think he was on the nose when he wrote it. Now if I was going to set up a games store today. If I was going to advise somebody on setting up a games store today.

I'd say you needed at least 300 grand. And if you look at my coaching offer at the back of the book, you'll see that's at least 400,000 pounds. And to really succeed I'd say probably 500,000. Because a lot of stuff now quite frankly costs a lot more

We have seen a huge amount of inflation since 2018. It is now much more important to advertise online than the budget that Gary gives it back in 2018. The games market has, as I've said before matured. There is more competition. Also unless your job happens to be running Google ads for somebody and you're you are actually good at it. Because most people I've seen who have come and offered to run Google ads for me aren't actually that good.

Then you will have to spend a huge amount of money to learn how to run Google ads.

Like everything else worth doing. Advertising online is pay to learn. For some things in life the payment to learn is just time. For online advertising it's time, money and effort. I'd want at least £75K preferably £100k for advertising and marketing in the first 12 months to have a hope of making the store successful. And that's me with all my experience. Without that experience you can double that amount.

Also takes into account the amount of money you need to pay yourself is more than it would be in 2018. Because cost of living has risen.

In terms of money, you're not doing this on a shoestring budget at least not successfully, at least not in a way that you'll still be there in a couple of years

So please do the maths, do the budgeting, figure it out yourself. Remember that you'll need to pay yourself a wage remember, that inflation is still high. And you'll have to take into account the amount of money you have in the bank decreases in value over time.

And decide if you have the money to do this.

Location

If you're running a "normal business" then general business advice to you would be whatever you want to do, you're going to find somewhere somebody is successfully running that business and you set up there. Because that shows you that there was a market for it. And that's a relatively sound piece of advice.

But if you then consider a few businesses that are more like running a games store you'll see that that's not sound advice.

Let's take a few other businesses as an example. Barbers, nail salons and vape shops.

If you live in a reasonable sized town you will have seen this play out over the years.

There are a number of barbers an area can support. And you'll have a period of time where there are that many in operation.

Then someone follows the general business advice and opens another barbers.

And what will happen is one, or more, barbers will then go out of business in the next few months. And you can almost guarantee it will be the new barbers that closes.

Because the old ones already have their customers. And the new barber has to try and get them off them. That's hard work. It requires marketing skills, advertising skills. And the money to use both.

The new place probably doesn't have the money and certainly doesn't have the skills.

So they don't get the customers they need and they close down.

And this will be an almost continuous cycle in these businesses.

Because they all have a really low barrier to entry. So loads of people go into them thinking I want to run a business. Without doing the work they need to be successful.

Sound familiar?

If you're wondering. Most cities in the UK can sustain a maximum of 2 games stores. If there are already 2 where you live then forget setting up a third.

And if you don't live in a city. I've seen a few seaside towns that have made stores work. But then you'll get that weird seasonal cash flow situation going on.

Thinking you run a games store

This last week I have been an:

- Accountant
- Cleaner
- Counselor
- Marketer
- Copywriter
- Box packer
- Web designer

That's not an exhaustive list.

What I haven't been is a games store owner.

What most people think of as a games store owner is the bit they see me doing in the store. Sat behind the counter serving. I do that two days a week because I enjoy it. And because if I'm in the store it reduces the amount of work I can do for two days.

I should really pay someone else to do that part and spend the time working instead.

It's like looking at the tip of an iceberg and thinking that's the entire thing when most of it is below the surface and out of sight.

I know more than one person who have started their own store because I make it look easy. They've all failed.

And every other successful store owner you speak to will tell you the same story.

The games store owner public perception bit looks easy. The real work is behind the scenes.

And there's a lot of it.

So there you have it.

Not every one of my 16 reasons games stores fail. But a decent whack of them. And if you see yourself in any of them, please think twice before setting up a store.

And if you've read them and for some reason haven't been put off. Then see my coaching offer at the back of the book.

And yes. I'm serious about the price.

Business is Boring

This is a special bonus chapter. Not just for you if you run or are looking to run a games store. If I haven't put you off already.

But it's also if you run any other business.

This is a summing up of the most important lesson I've learned over the last seven and a half years of running a business.

And it is both a very simple, but also very profound lesson. One that I still haven't mastered one that still runs counterintuitive to everything we've been brainwashed into thinking about businesses from TV, from reading books and from how society indoctrinates us.

And here's the secret.

Business is meant to be boring.

Now you may read that and go "What the hell's he talking about?" But let me let me explain. Fundamentally the act of doing business is very boring.

Let's take my business for example.

This week, I have done the exact same processes that I did last week and the week before and the week before that. And for some of them they go back only a few months. For some they go back six months or more and for I've done them for years.

Because the art of doing business is the art of doing things that are measurable and repeatable over and over again.

So for instance, this week, I have put in orders with my suppliers.

I've done that since the first week we opened. There is a process to doing it. I follow that process week in and week out. Eventually I will reach a stage, and this probably has more to do with my unwillingness to delegate it than it does to the level of growth we're currently at.

But eventually I will reach a stage where I will pass that process onto someone else. And it will be a very regimented process. I already have it written down as a series of steps and it will get passed on and it will become someone else's job on a Monday to do the Games Workshop order. To follow the process on a Tuesday to order from somewhere else.

And they will then continue doing the ordering in the way that I've set it out, in the way that I have created the process right up until the point they either come to me with a better way of doing it. Or they leave the company and someone else takes it on.

It is very, very boring

But it is 100% effective.

In my business I email to my customers every single day. If you're on my email subscription list, you'll get at least one email from me daily.

Those emails are interesting, entertaining, and will always sell you something. The process of getting those emails to you is incredibly boring. I write an email every single day. That is the process. Is there is more to it than that. Yes.

There's a hell of a lot more to it than that. That I won't go into here because it's the parts that make me the money. But the process is a very boring process. It's a consistent process. Business is meant to be boring.

The only times in the last seven years when business hasn't been boring is the first year where I set it up before I figured out and started putting the processes down. When we first opened the original store, when we moved into the biggest store and then when the pandemic hit. And those four points in time all share something in common.

A huge period of uncertainty, a huge likelihood of failure, vast levels of risk.

Boring no. Would I like to do any of them again?

Absolutely not. I'll take boring any day!

When a business is boring it continues to grow, if you've set it up properly, at a reasonably steady rate.

You can take yourself out or parts of it and put somebody else in. So I can delegate out the ordering. I can't and wouldn't want to delegate out the daily emails. That's far too important for me.

But you can do this delegation for most of the day to day running of the business.

And of course, if I ever wanted to. I can sell the business. Because the business itself is a series of processes And if I haven't already, I can easily sit down, write down those processes and pass them over to somebody else.

If you look at businesses that have been brought out by somebody else you'll actually find quite a high failure rate. It's not unusual for somebody to buy a business that has been up and running for 5, 10, 20 years has been really successful for that time.

And then somebody else buys it. And six months later it's belly up. It's completely failing or it's shutting down. Indeed I know more than one person who has sold a business for huge amounts of money and then brought it back six to twelve months later for pennies on the pound. Because the person who's brought it off them has run the business into the ground.

And then you look and ask how has someone managed to do that?

Well, the answer is simple. The new person came in. They looked at all the stuff that the existing owner had in place. They said to themselves, consciously or unconsciously, well, that's really boring.

And then they thought I can do it better. And then they proceeded to destroy the business. Because they know best. And they don't need to follow all those boring processes that have been laid out and followed for years.

You can even see this in the corporate world. Where a new chief executive comes into a really big company and runs it into the ground.

Because what should happen is the new person comes in, looks around and goes, right well that's really boring. Okay, let's run the really boring stuff for 12 to 18 months.

And in that 12 to 18 months. They may very well find something else and go oh, that could work. Try it, realise it does work, that it increases your sales. That increases your turnover. It increases your profit and start doing that.

But then the moment you start doing it, you codify it. You make it something that you do regularly. It then becomes a boring process again because business is meant to be boring.

And the reason why I write this is because throughout the book, I've written about personality types. Wherever I've written about how not to run a games store, most of the time what I've been writing about is individual personality traits that will completely scupper your ability to run a store

This is another one of those overarching traits.

If you need to be constantly distracted. If you have trained yourself to have the attention span of two minutes by spending all of your free time and most of the time when you're allegedly working on tick tock on other social media. You will massively struggle to run a business

Why?

Because running a business is a very boring thing to do. It's about figuring out a load of processes doing those processes, in the order that they need to be done. When they need to be done, how they need to be done.

Repeating that over and over again. And knowing that some of those processes may in and of themselves require a large attention to detail and significantly more than two minutes at a time of concentration.

And I know if you're reading this and you've got this idea of running of a game store. And you keep on coming back to this chapter because you keep on getting distracted and wandering off. Then it'll be very easy to write me off for some random old guy who clearly doesn't know what I'm talking about.

But this has been shown over and over again. And you can go back and you can look for as long as there are records and you will see that this is how a business runs.

There's a curse in more than one language. That essentially translates to May you live in interesting times. And the reason why that is a curse is because interesting is not successful.

Interesting is not having predictable outcomes. It's not knowing where your next paycheck is going to come from. Or, more importantly if you have staff. Where their next paycheck is going to come from.

Interesting is not knowing how you're going to pay the bills. You do not want an interesting business.

An interesting business keeps you awake at night.

If you want to know about interesting businesses go and speak to all those people who have had games stores that failed. They will have had a very interesting business experience whilst it was in operation.

It will be very interesting that constant struggle to keep the lights on and the doors open.

That is the type interesting you do not want to experience.

My main reason for writing the how not to run a games store parts of this book is because I've seen people go through that and I'll be honest.

I would not wish it on my worst enemy.

It is not a fun experience.

It is not an experience you will get out of without emotional and financial scars.

And, because of the levels of stress involved. Because of people not thinking correctly because of the worry. I can show you more than one person who has had that type of business with very real physical scars.

Because they haven't lifted something properly. They've not been paying attention when they've been using a hobby knife. Or they've been worrying about how they're going to pay this month's rent on the drive home and crashed.

This is why I say you do not want an interesting business.

You want a boring business.

Now as I alluded to earlier in this chapter my business for lack of a better way of describing it has become more boring over time.

The longer it's in operation, the more things I find that work, the more processes I find that by doing them I get the results I want.

And this is worth mentioning just in case you're an incredibly literal person

When I first, let's go with the process of me writing a daily email.

It's the one that realistically you're the least likely to attempt to copy

And also the one that you can't copy unless you've invested the time, money and effort that I have into learning how to do it properly.

When I first started them. When I first started writing my daily email it was interesting.

But by the time I realised that the information I'd learned. The information I spent very good money to learn, was actually correct. That I'd validated that information, showing to myself that it was indeed something that was worth me doing.

The process of writing a daily email by that point, had become a process. It had become boring, essentially a tick box for me. Have I sent out an email today? Tick, good, no tick, bad. Sit down and write one.

So it started out as one thing that was interesting and is now something that's boring.

Don't get me wrong. There is a creative, artistic side to writing daily. In the same way there's a creative, artistic side to writing this book and I very much enjoy the process of both.

But the reason for doing it, the way I do it, the way I structure it. That's all codified into a process and it's an incredibly boring thing

Occasionally I'll do business coaching for other people. And when I do this is the process I go through. How can I make your business more profitable by making it more boring?

Because a boring business is a business you can step out from if that's what you want to do.

That you can sell if that's what you want to do.

A boring businesses is a business that gives you the freedom to bolt on other processes to make the business even more boring, but also, even more successful and even more profitable.

So if you are interested in being bored in business check out my offer on the next page.

Coaching Offer

The rest of this book has hopefully been entertaining, a worthwhile read and something that you have enjoyed whether you're looking at running your own games store. Just wanted to know how we got started, or even you have your own business and have been interested in some of my business ideas.

What follows is a blatant sales pitch.

So if you don't run your own business. If you have no intention of running your own business, you can probably skip these final few pages.

And I will say goodbye to you now. And also remind you that if you haven't already, sign up for the extra bonuses.

Now I'm assuming anybody still reading is either considering setting up their own games store or they run their own business?

I will get the games store people out the way first.

There is a phrase amongst coaches that you probably won't have heard before, which is that there's often more money in keeping secrets than in sharing them.

By which I mean if I lay out exactly how I run Leodis Games, you can take that and you can follow it. And if you're able to follow instructions, if you're willing to be bored by setting up processes and following those processes. Within a few months you could legitimately be one of my competitors.

I clearly have very little reason for wanting that to happen.

So here's my offer to you.

You get in contact with me. You tell me that you're willing to pay me £100,000 and I will sit down with you and show you exactly how to run a games store, the entire thing. I'll even mentor you for a few months whilst you get it sorted.

And trust me when I say you are getting a bargain.

Because it has definitely cost me a lot more than 100 grand to get to where I am now.

And if you go and you speak to any other successful games store and the emphasis here was on successful. They will tell you that it's taken them over 100 grand worth of mistakes to get them to where they are.

And I will offer you that shortcut.

Well, I may offer you that shortcut.

If you get in contact and you based anywhere near West Yorkshire, expect me to tell you to go jump off a cliff. Because this is my area. This is my store and I will have no qualms about putting you out of business if you try and set up on my doorstep.

So that's my offer to you. The fellow games store owner, the potential fellow game store owner.

Now to the rest of you reading this assuming that you don't want to run a games store.

That you run your own business in a completely different sector.

Or you're looking at setting up your own games company and producing games or anything else on the business side of things.

I do on occasion offer business coaching.

If after having read this book and if you skipped all the way to the back and just read this. I would highly recommend you go back and reread the book first.

And if you have read from cover to cover I highly recommend you go back and read it at least once more before you make this decision.

If you would like me to do some business coaching with you, and thanks to the magic of the internet you can be anywhere in the world.

Then for pennies on the pound on my games store price we could possibly sit down and work together.

And this could be very useful for a range of things from general business advice and coaching, through to marketing and setting up and running Google & Facebook ads.

To find out more drop me a message to admin@ leodisgames.com and put Business Coaching in the title and we'll talk

Johnny B

Leodis is, in my opinion is Leeds premier gaming shop. Neil has an excellent hobby space and shop. The space is clean, bright, and welcoming Cool in the summer (AC) and warm in the winter. Neil also has plenty of events, tournaments, and leagues available. Plus a great physical shop with plenty on offer!

Kappa Coco

Feel very lucky to have this place on my doorstep. Excellent selection of 40K and AOS models and citadel paints. Very friendly staff who let you just get on with browsing without hassling you.

Toby R

Easily booked a table online. Had an awesome selection of terrain and lots of tables for a 40k game against my friend. Owner was very friendly. Amazing place, highly recommended.

Adam S

Great place to play tabletop games like 40k. Friendly and helpful staff, clean facilities and free parking. Good discount on various game types and a large community of players to have games with. Fantastic all round.

Sam D

I've been visiting this shop fairly regularly over the past few months, and it's a great shop with great gaming tables. I've had a great time here, but I'll share my family's experience at Leodis. I attended a 40K GT at the weekend. My wife came in with my 2 year old son, so he could see me set up, and have a look around. After I got back from the tournament, my wife informed me the TO had offered to get my wife a hot drink, and a little table and some dice set up so my son could pretend he was playing. They both had plans, so she had to decline, but this sort of service is above and beyond. I can understand how, on a busy Sunday, with a packed tournament, it could be annoying to have a small child around, but making my wife and child feel welcome like this is amazing.

Giles G

Great place for gaming and hobbying. Staff know their stuff and are really helpful. Chance to get a decent cup of coffee there is a definite bonus. Superb community. Plenty of parking.

J Holland

The definition of a friendly local gaming store. Neil has an awesome place along with the rest of his staff and everyone who games. 40K alone has a slow grow league, a competition league and then multiple GT style comps through the year!

Kieran G

Great atmosphere, store manager is a lovely dude, so is the owner. Better than a lot of chain game shops. Great stock for MTG and Warhammer. Plenty of tables and space.

Simon T

A great store, either for in shop gaming or online, but get there in person if you can always games going it seems. Great for DnD, boardgaming, MTG, wargaming, card games, necromunda, SW legion, always seems to be a bit of everything going on!

Mark M

Fantastic friendly shop and staff. Loads of stock (sometimes the mercy of Games Workshop of course!). Great range of products, not just GW. Fab gaming space inside with loads of terrain for the gaming tables. Also, good coffee and snacks for when you are playing games on those tables!

Chris G

A lovey community based friendly local gaming store. Have never had an issue with any of my purchases, whether online or in store. During the COVID disruption in 2020 they managed to keep deliveries going and clearly communicated the delays. Great to pop into for a browse or game.

James W

Brilliant throughout lockdown. Great availability throughout the shop with a genuinely nice owner who will always try his best to help you. Replies fast to any queries ive had. I used to live near the shop so popping in was no hassle but with moving I have had stuff ordered, always dispatched promptly.

Mark T

Really friendly store, perfect place to enjoy gaming and also a go to stockist. Always happy to give advice and answer any questions. Super smooth ordering and always fast delivery.

Printed in Great Britain
by Amazon

28784312R00079